BEST OF JOHN DENVER

Silver Anniversary Edition

EASY PIANO

Management: Advent Management Corp.
Music Engraving by Gordon Hallberg
Production: Daniel Rosenbaum/Rana Bernhardt
Art Direction: Rosemary Cappa-Jenkins
Director of Music: Mark Phillips

Photography by John Russell

Sunshine On My Shoulders

Words by John Denver
Music by John Denver, Mike Taylor and Dick Kniss

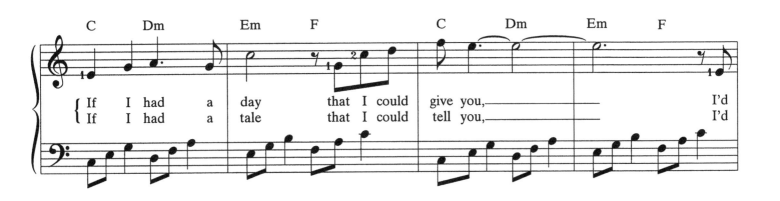

If I had a day that I could give you,_____ I'd
If I had a tale that I could tell you, I'd

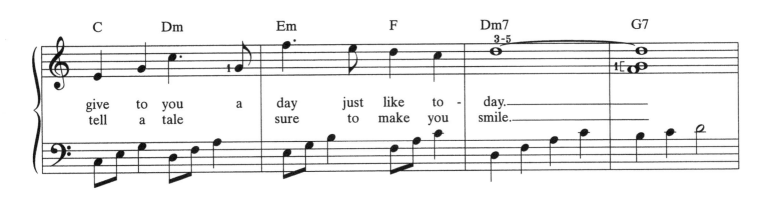

give to you a day just like to - day._____
tell a tale sure to make you smile._____

If I had a song that I could sing for you,_____ I'd
If I had a wish that I could wish for you,_____ I'd

2nd time, D.C. al Fine

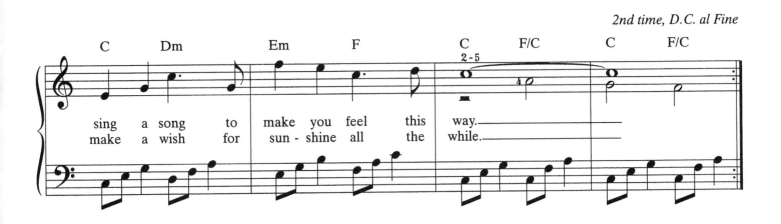

sing a song to make you feel this way._____
make a wish for sun - shine all the while._____

Rocky Mountain High

Words by John Denver
Music by John Denver and Mike Taylor

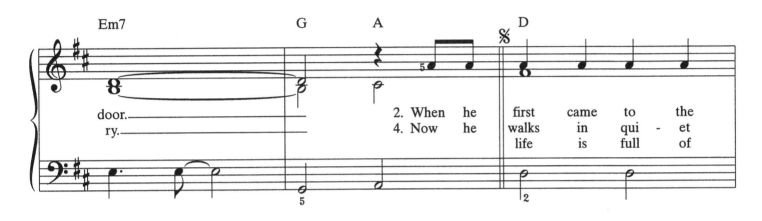

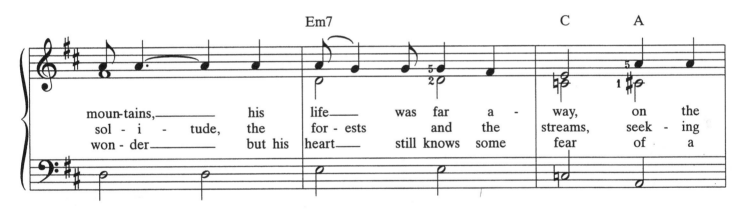

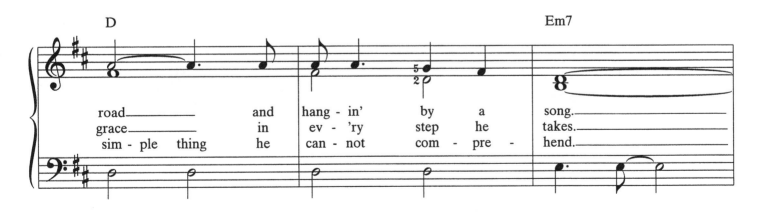

seen it rain - in' fire in the sky.___ { The shad-ow from the
I know he'd be a

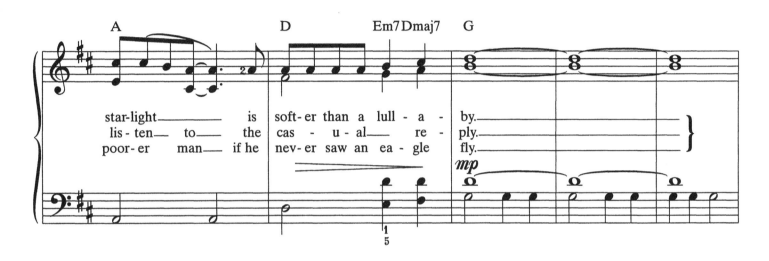

star-light___ is soft - er than a lull - a - by.___
lis - ten___ to___ the cas - u - al re - ply.___
poor - er man___ if he nev - er saw an ea - gle fly.___

mp

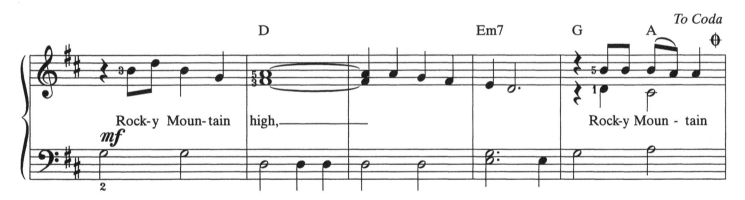

To Coda

Rock-y Moun-tain high,___ Rock-y Moun - tain
mf

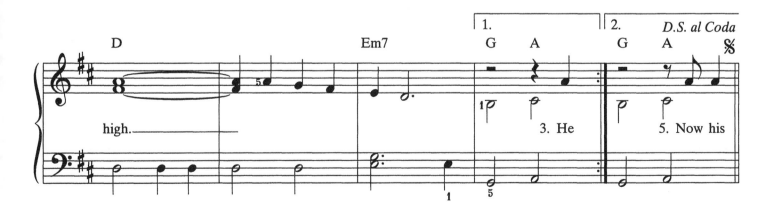

1.   2. *D.S. al Coda*

high.___   3. He   5. Now his

Take Me Home, Country Roads

Words and Music by
John Denver, Bill Danoff and Taffy Nivert

Moderately

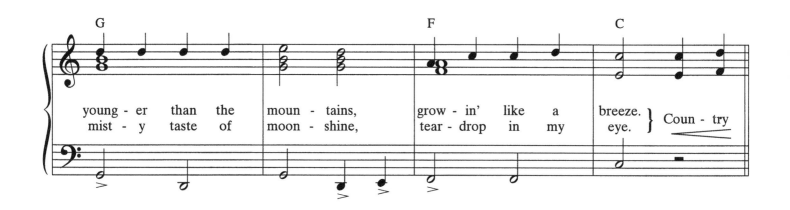

young - er than the moun - tains, grow - in' like a breeze. } Coun - try
mist - y taste of moon - shine, tear - drop in my eye.

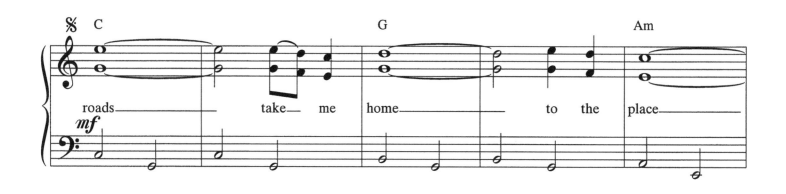

roads_____ take_ me home_____ to the place_____

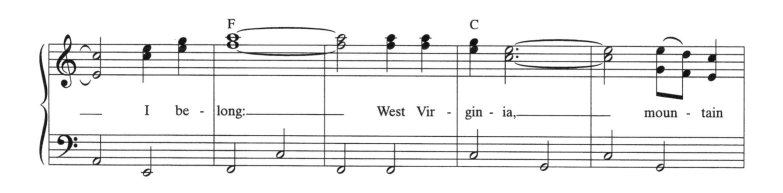

_____ I be - long:_____ West Vir - gin - ia,_____ moun - tain

3rd time to Coda

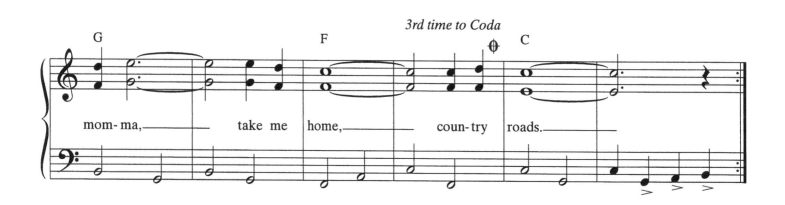

mom - ma,_____ take me home,_____ coun - try roads._____

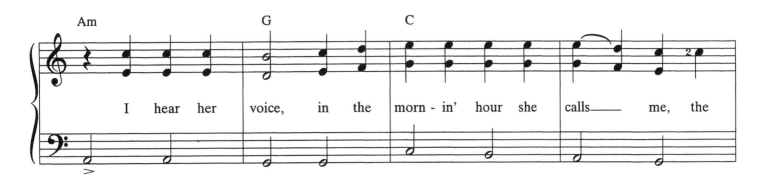

I hear her voice, in the morn-in' hour she calls___ me, the

ra - di - o re - minds me of my home far a - way. And

driv-in' down the road I get a feel-in' that I should have been home

D.S. al Coda

yes-ter-day,___ yes-ter-day.___ Coun-try

Coda

roads.___

Annie's Song

Words and Music by
John Denver

rain._____
arms._____

Like a storm in the
Let me lay down be-

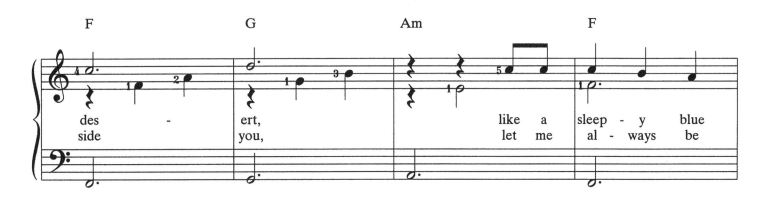

des — ert,
side you,

like a sleep - y blue
let me al - ways be

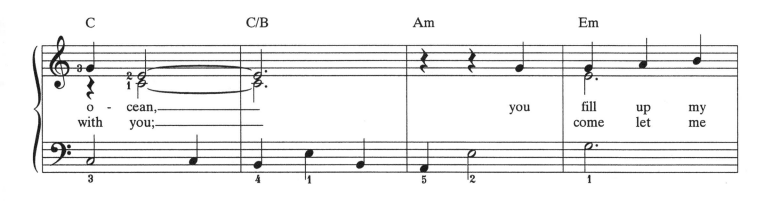

o - cean,_____
with you;_____

you fill up my
come let me

To Coda $\oplus$

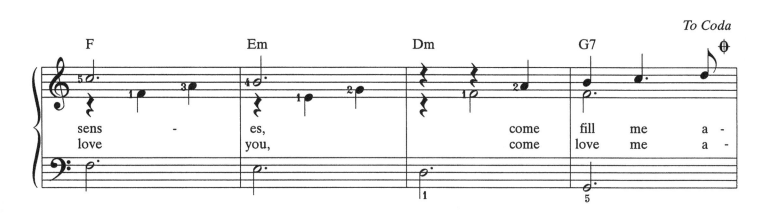

sens — es,
love you,

come fill me a -
come love me a -

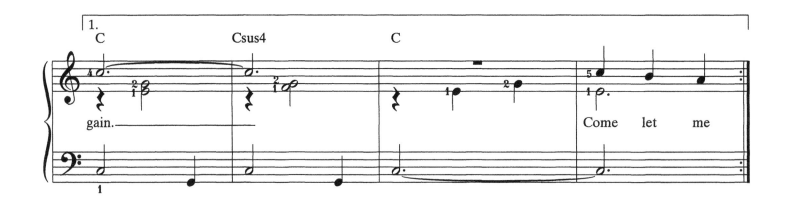

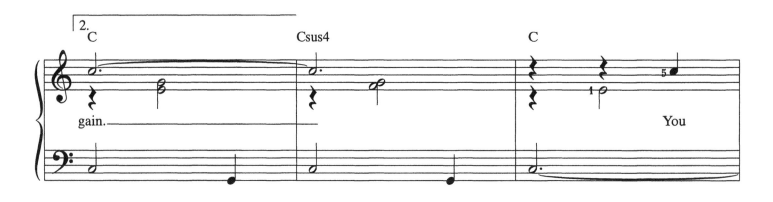

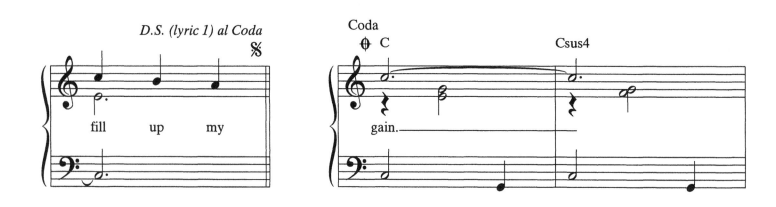

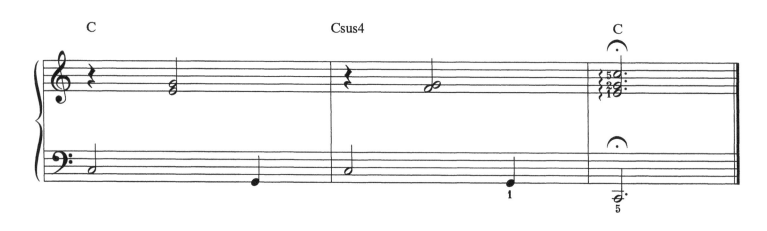

I'm Sorry

Words and Music by
John Denver

Moderately

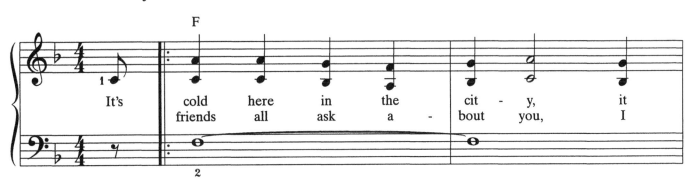

It's cold here in the cit - y, it
friends all ask a - bout you, I

al - ways seems that way, and I've been think - in' a -
say you're do - in' fine. I ex - pect to hear

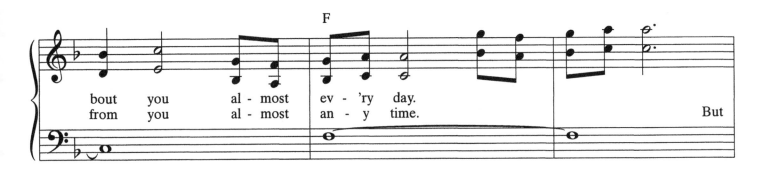

bout you al - most ev - 'ry day.
from you al - most an - y time. But

Think - in' a - bout the good times,
they all know I'm cry - in', that

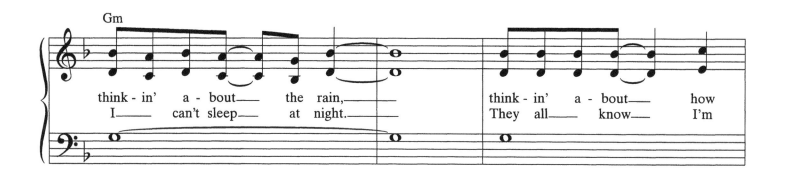

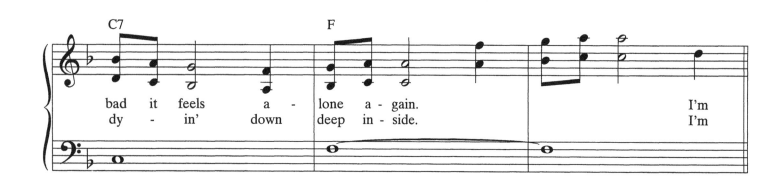

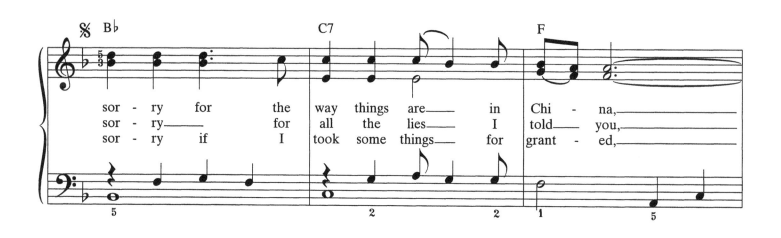

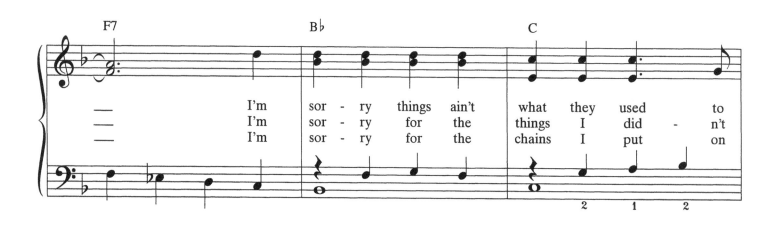

Thank God I'm A Country Boy

Words and Music by
John Martin Sommers

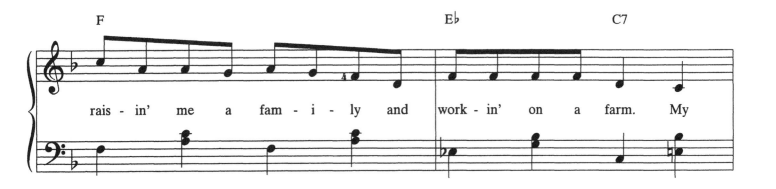

rais - in' me a fam - i - ly and work - in' on a farm. My

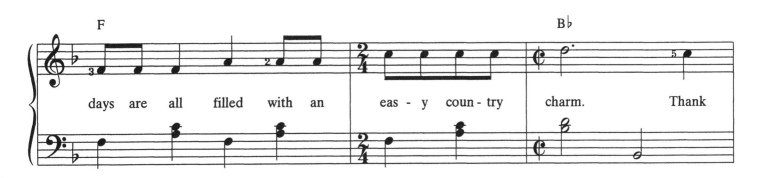

days are all filled with an eas - y coun - try charm. Thank

Chorus

God I'm a coun - try boy. Well, I got me a fine wife, I

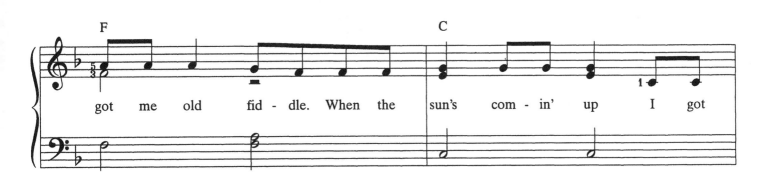

got me old fid - dle. When the sun's com - in' up I got

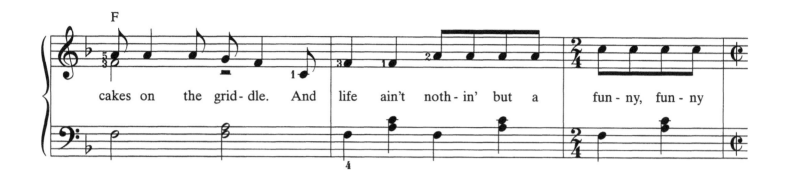

cakes on the grid-dle. And life ain't noth-in' but a fun-ny, fun-ny

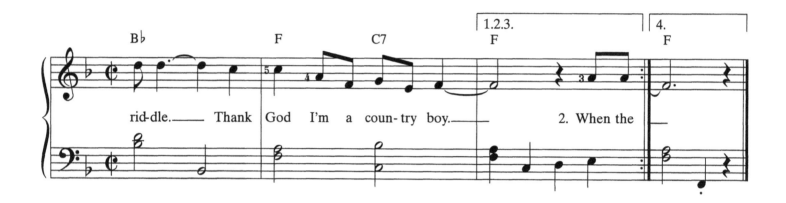

rid-dle.___ Thank God I'm a coun-try boy.___ 2. When the

Additional Lyrics

2. When the work's all done and the sun's settin' low
I pull out my fiddle and I rosin up the bow.
But the kids are asleep so I keep it kinda low.
Thank God I'm a country boy.
I'd play "Sally Goodin' " all day if I could,
But the Lord and my wife wouldn't take it very good.
So I fiddle when I can and I work when I should.
Thank God I'm a country boy. *(To Chorus)*

3. I wouldn't trade my life for diamonds or jewels,
I never was one of them money-hungry fools.
I'd rather have my fiddle and my farmin' tools.
Thank God I'm a country boy.
Yeah, city folk drivin' in a black limousine,
A lotta sad people thinkin' that's mighty keen.
Well folks, let me tell you now exactly what I mean:
I thank God I'm a country boy. *(To Chorus)*

4. Well, my fiddle was my daddy's till the day he died,
And he took me by the hand and held me close to his side.
He said, "Live a good life and play my fiddle with pride,
And thank God you're a country boy."
My daddy taught me young how to hunt and how to whittle,
He taught me how to work and play a tune on the fiddle.
He taught me how to love and how to give just a little.
Thank God I'm a country boy. *(To Chorus)*

Back Home Again

Words and Music by
John Denver

way,   the   whin - in'   of——   his   wheels   just   makes   it

cold - er.   He's an   hour   a - way   from
                                                 all   the news   to
                                                 sweet   - est   thing   I

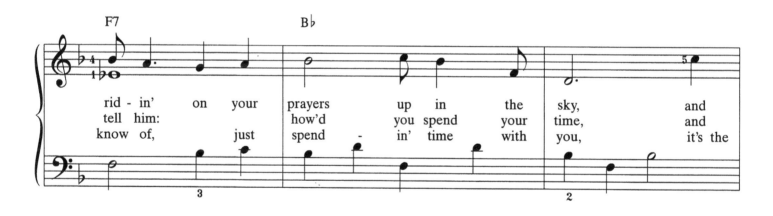

rid - in'   on   your   prayers   up   in   the   sky,   and
tell him: how'd   you spend   your   time,   and
know of,   just   spend - in' time   with   you,   it's the

ten   days   on——   the   road——   are bare - ly   gone.——
what's   the   lat - est   thing——   the neigh-bors   say?——
lit - tle   things——   that   make——   a house a   home,——

There's a fire softly burn-ing,
And your moth-er called last Fri-day,
like a fire softly burn-ing and

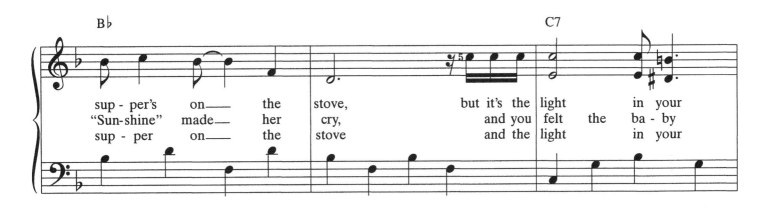

sup-per's on the stove, but it's the light in your
"Sun-shine" made her cry, and you felt the ba-by
sup-per on the stove and the light in your

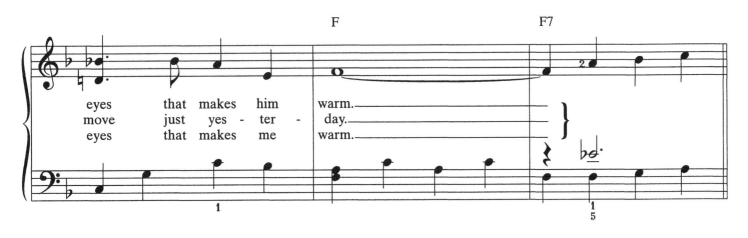

eyes that makes him warm.
move just yes-ter-day.
eyes that makes me warm.

Chorus

Hey, it's good to be back home a-gain.

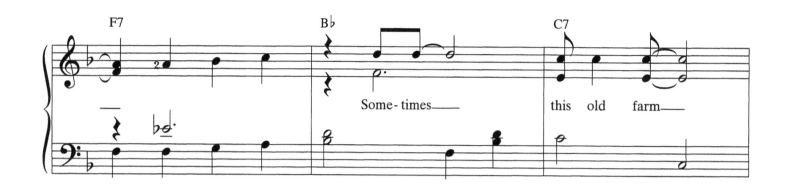

Some-times———— this old farm————

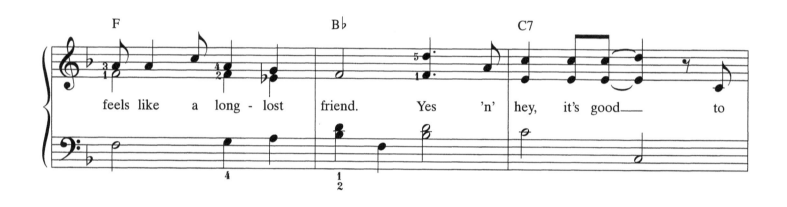

feels like a long - lost friend. Yes 'n' hey, it's good———— to

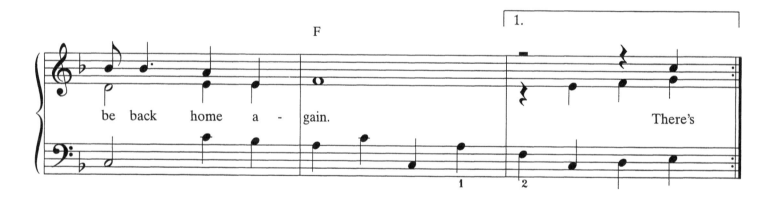

be back home a - gain.

1.

There's

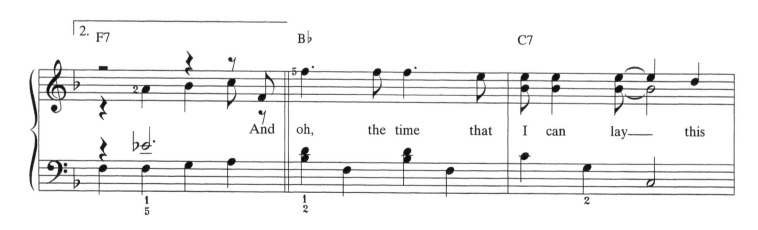

2. And oh, the time that I can lay———— this

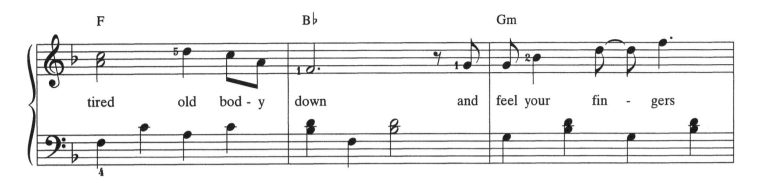

tired   old   bod - y   down   and   feel your   fin - gers

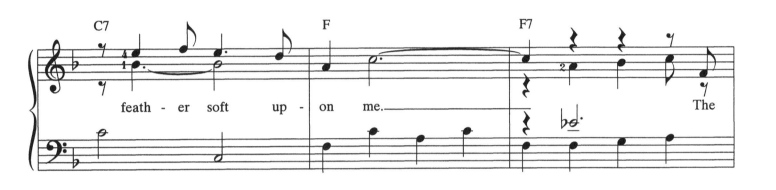

feath - er   soft   up - on   me._____   The

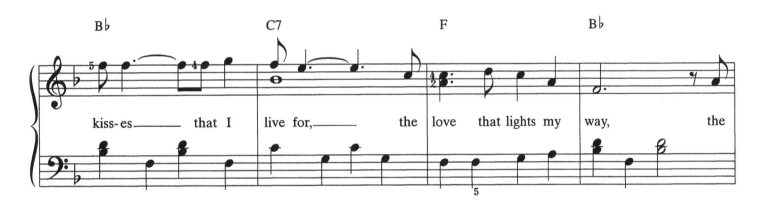

kiss-es_____ that I   live for,_____   the   love   that lights my   way,   the

D.S. and fade on Chorus

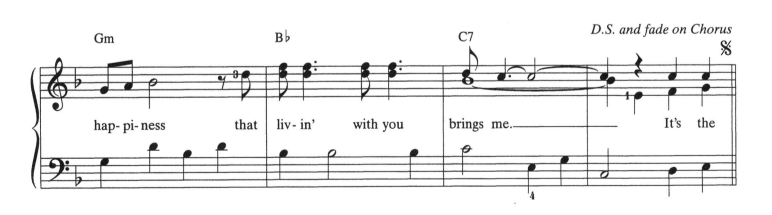

hap- pi- ness   that   liv- in'   with you   brings me._____   It's the

Goodbye Again

Words and Music by
John Denver

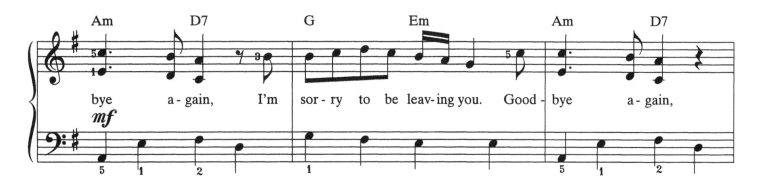

bye   a - gain,   I'm   sor - ry   to   be   leav-ing you.   Good - bye   a - gain,

mf

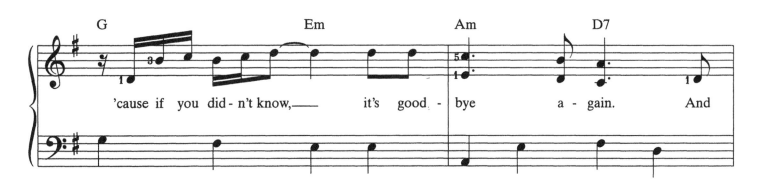

'cause   if   you   did - n't know,_____   it's   good - bye   a - gain.   And

To Coda ⊕

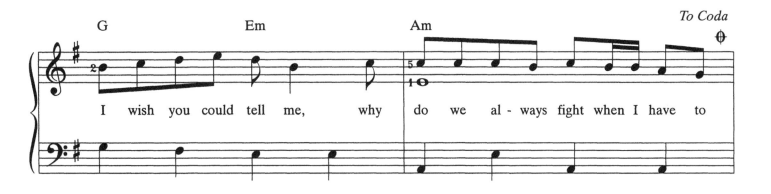

I   wish   you   could   tell   me,   why   do   we   al - ways   fight   when   I   have   to

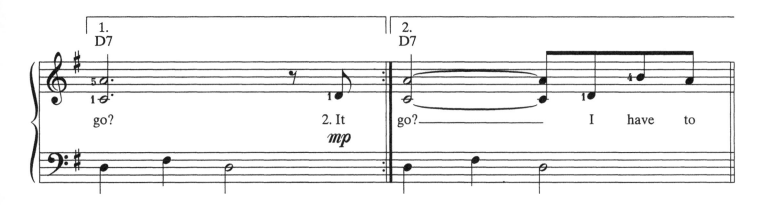

1.
D7

go?   2. It

mp

2.
D7

go?_____   I   have   to

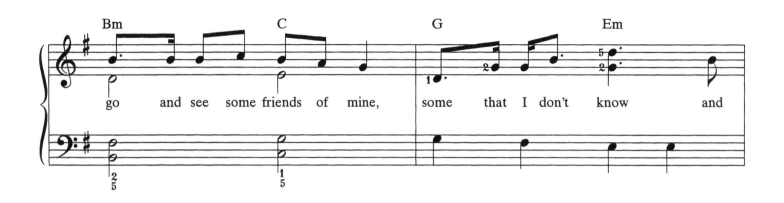

go and see some friends of mine, some that I don't know and

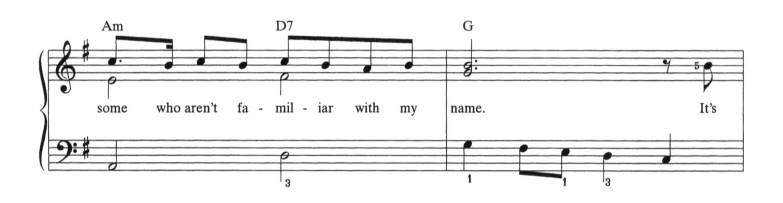

some who aren't fa - mil - iar with my name. It's

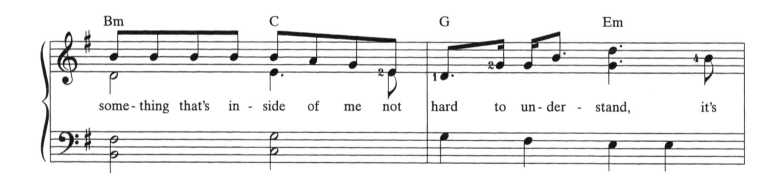

some - thing that's in - side of me not hard to un - der - stand, it's

D.S. al Coda

an - y - one___ who'll lis - ten to me sing. 3. And

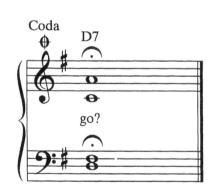

go?

My Sweet Lady

Words and Music by
John Denver

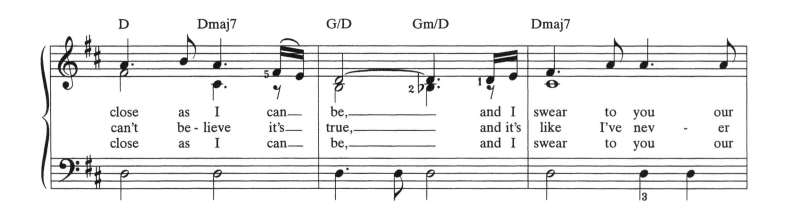

close as I can— be,_____ and I swear to you our
can't be- lieve it's— true,_____ and it's like I've nev - er
close as I can— be,_____ and I swear to you our

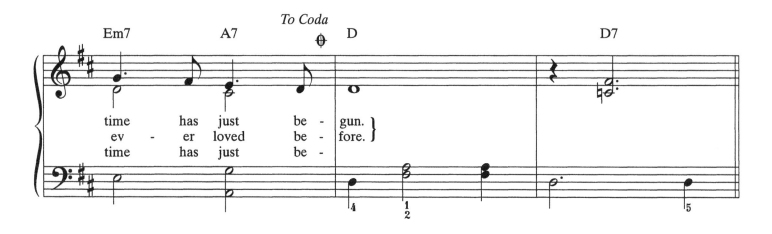

To Coda ⊕

time has just be - gun. ⎫
ev - er loved be - fore. ⎬
time has just be - ⎭

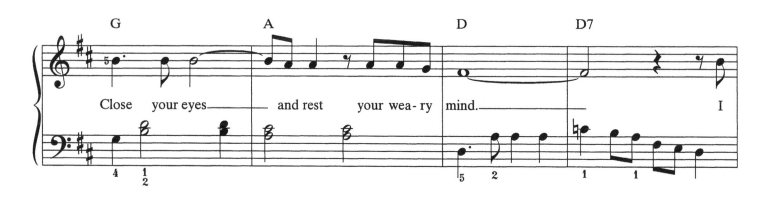

Close your eyes____ and rest your wea-ry mind.____ I

prom-ise I will stay right— here be - side— you._____

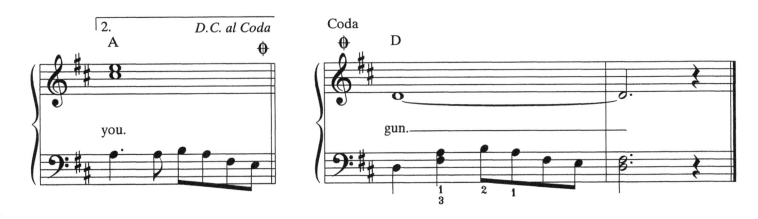

Fly Away

Words and Music by
John Denver

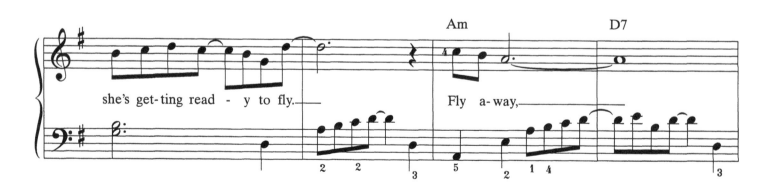

To Coda

Am D7 G

D7sus4

G

Life in the cit - y can make you cra - zy for
look - ing for lov - ers and chil - dren play - ing, for she's

sounds of the sand— and the sea.
look - ing for signs— of the spring. She

D7sus4 G

Life in a high - rise can
lis - tens for laugh - ter and

make you hun - gry for things that you can't— e - ven see.—
sounds of danc - ing, she lis - tens for an - y old thing.—

Perhaps Love

Words and Music by
John Denver

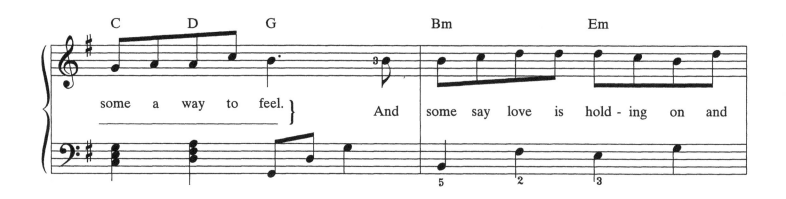

some a way to feel. And some say love is hold - ing on and

some say let - ting go. And some say love is ev - 'ry - thing,

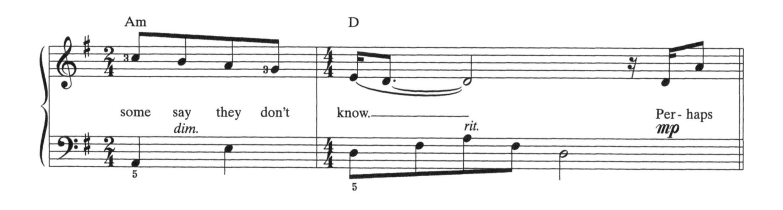

some say they don't know. Per - haps
dim.   rit.   mp

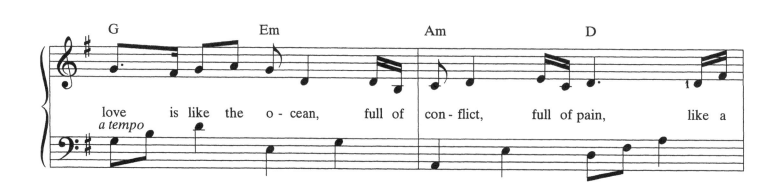

love is like the o - cean, full of con - flict, full of pain, like a
a tempo

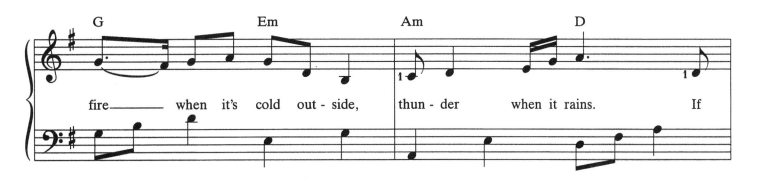

fire_____ when it's cold out - side, thun - der when it rains. If

I should live for - ev - er and all my dreams come true, my

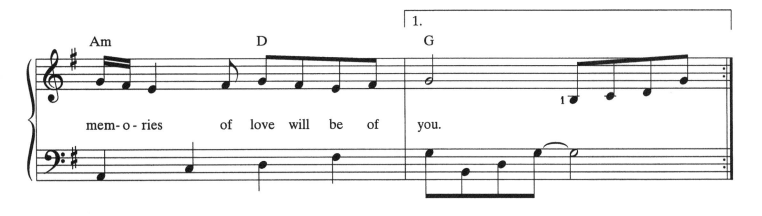

1.

mem - o - ries of love will be of you.

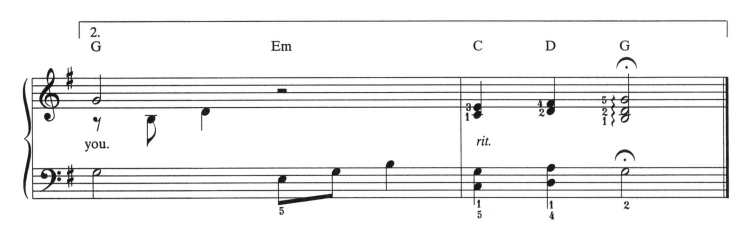

2.

you.

rit.

Follow Me

Words and Music by
John Denver

Moderately fast

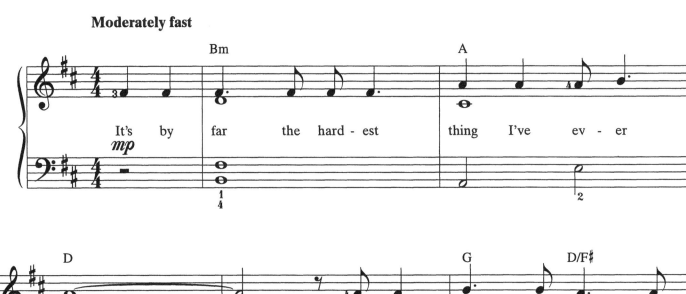

It's by far the hard-est thing I've ev-er

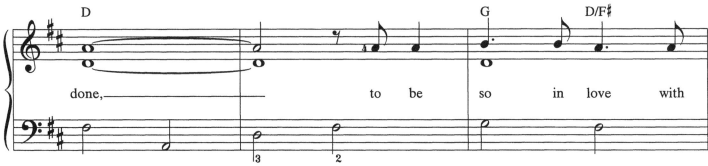

done, _____ to be so in love with

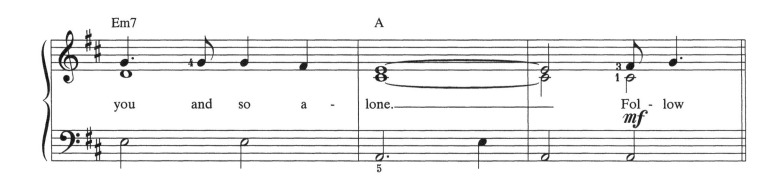

you and so a - lone. _____ Fol - low

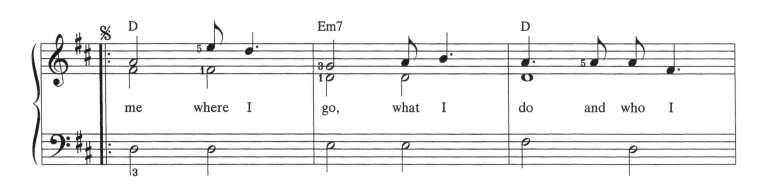

me where I go, what I do and who I

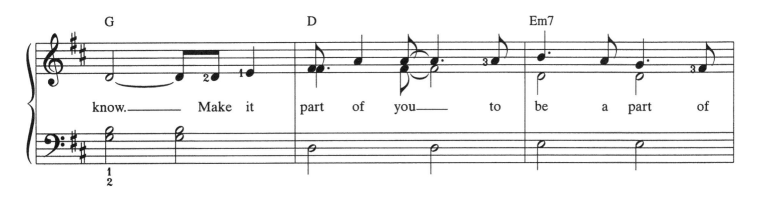

know._____ Make it part of you_____ to be a part of

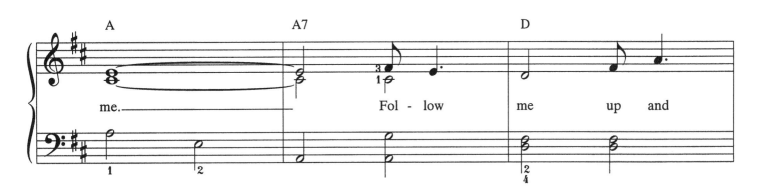

me._____ Fol - low me up and

down, all_____ the way and all a - round.

To Coda ⊕

Take my hand_____ and say you'll fol - low

me._____ It's long been on my

You see, I'd like to share my

mp

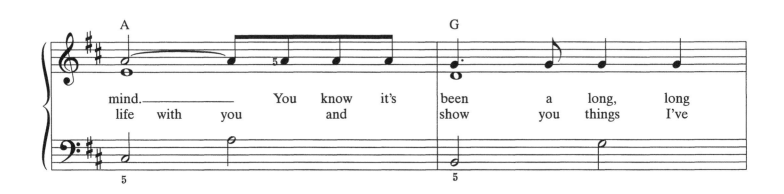

mind._____ You know it's been a long, long

life with you and show you things I've

time. I'll try to find the way that I can

seen, places that I'm going to,_____

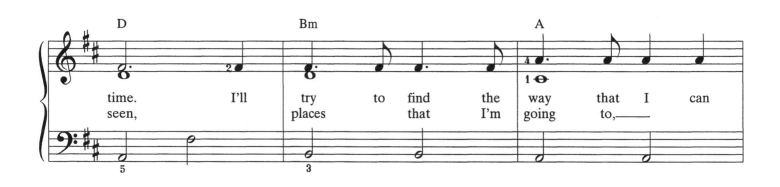

make you un - der - stand_____ the way I feel a -

places where_____ I've been,_____ to have you there be -

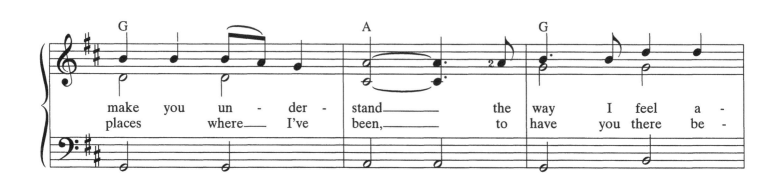

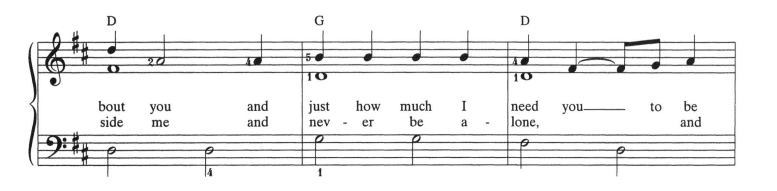

bout you and just how much I need you_____ to be
side me and nev - er be a - lone, and

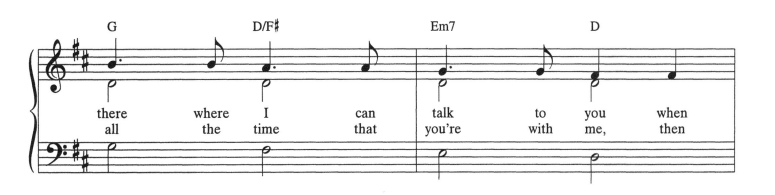

there where I can talk to you when
all the time that you're with me, then

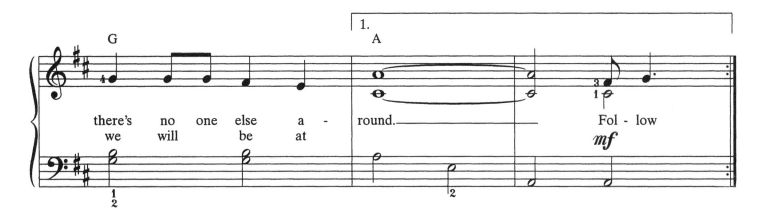

1.

there's no one else a - round._____ Fol - low
we will be at

mf

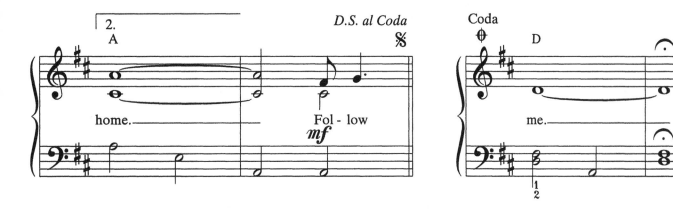

2.

D.S. al Coda 𝄋

Coda

home._____ Fol - low
mf

me._____

For Baby (For Bobbie)

Words and Music by
John Denver

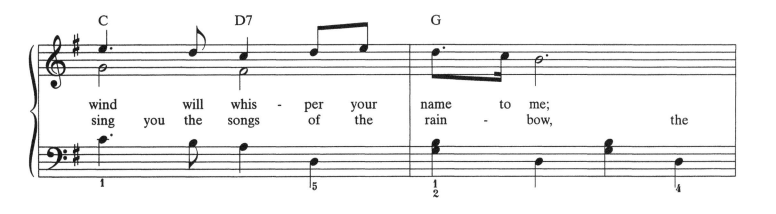

wind will whis - per your name to me;
sing you the songs of the rain - bow, the

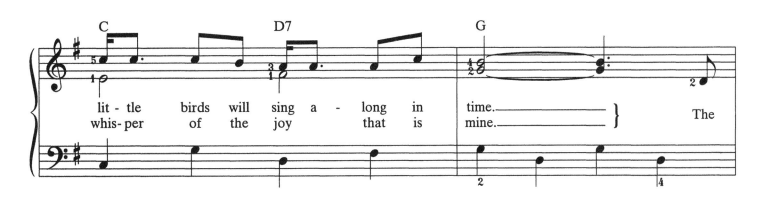

lit - tle birds will sing a - long in time._____
whis - per of the joy that is mine._____ } The

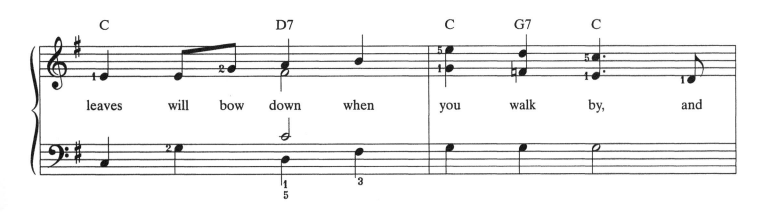

leaves will bow down when you walk by, and

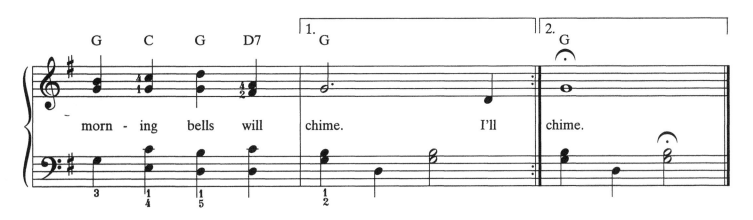

morn - ing bells will chime. I'll chime.

Grandma's Feather Bed

Words and Music by
Jim Connor

Moderately, in 2

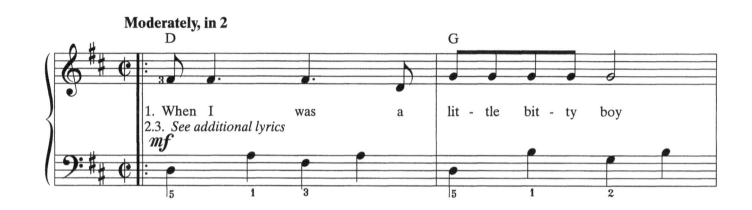

1. When I was a lit - tle bit - ty boy
2.3. *See additional lyrics*

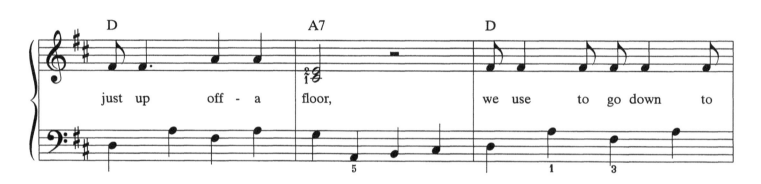

just up off - a floor, we use to go down to

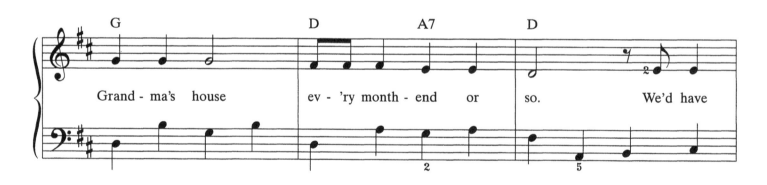

Grand - ma's house ev - 'ry month - end or so. We'd have

chick - en pie and coun - try ham ___ 'n' home - made but - ter on the

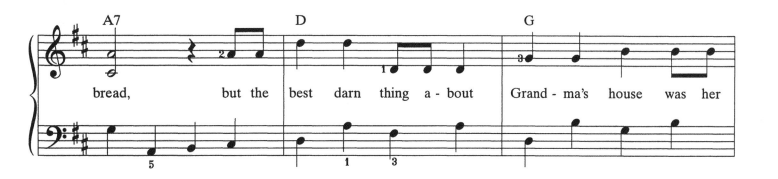

bread,   but the   best   darn   thing a - bout   Grand - ma's   house   was   her

Chorus

great   big——   feath - er   bed.   It   was   nine   feet   tall   and

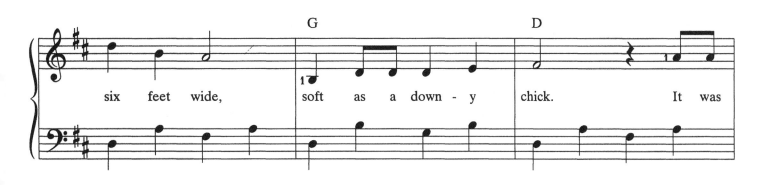

six   feet   wide,   soft   as   a   down - y   chick.   It   was

made from the feath-ers of   for - ty 'lev - en geese, took a   whole bolt of cloth for the

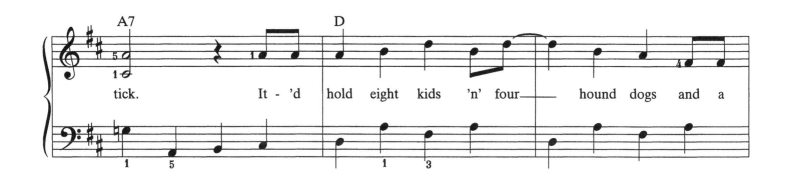

tick.   It - 'd hold eight kids 'n' four   hound dogs and a

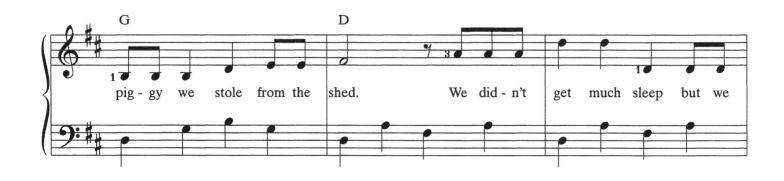

pig - gy we stole from the shed.   We did - n't get much sleep but we

To Coda

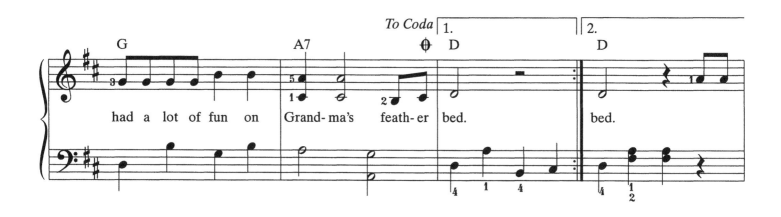

had a lot of fun on Grand- ma's feath- er bed.   bed.

D.C. al Coda

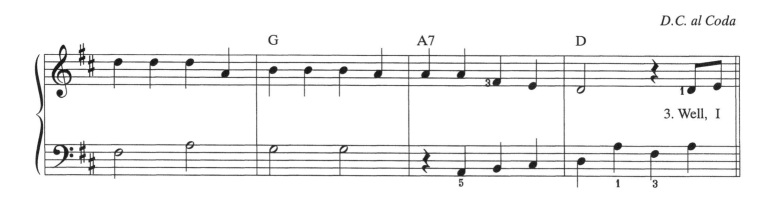

3. Well, I

bed. We did - n't get much sleep but we

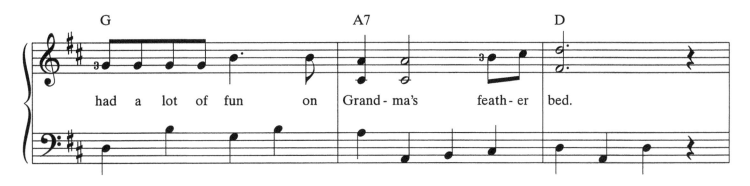

had a lot of fun on Grand - ma's feath - er bed.

Additional Lyrics

2. After supper we'd sit around the fire,
The old folks'd spit and chew.
Pa would talk about the farm and the war,
And Granny'd sing a ballad or two.
I'd sit and listen and watch the fire
Till the cobwebs filled my head.
Next thing I'd know I'd wake up in the mornin'
In the middle of the old feather bed. *(To Chorus)*

3. Well, I love my ma, I love my pa.
I love Granny and Grandpa too.
I been fishin' with my uncle, I rassled with my cousin,
I even kissed Aunt Loo ooo!
But if I ever had to make a choice.
I guess it oughta be said
That I'd trade 'em all plus the gal down the road
For Grandma's feather bed. *(To Chorus)*

Wild Montana Skies

Words and Music by
John Denver

Moderately, in 2

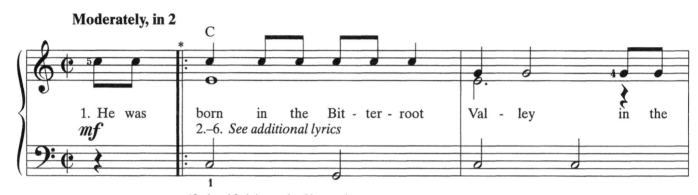

1. He was born in the Bit - ter - root Val - ley in the
2.–6. *See additional lyrics*

mf

*2nd and 3rd times, play Verse twice
before proceeding to Chorus.

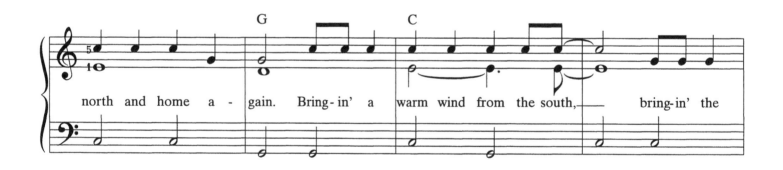

ear - ly morn - in' rain. Wild geese o - ver the wa - ter head - in'

north and home a - gain. Bring - in' a warm wind from the south,___ bring - in' the

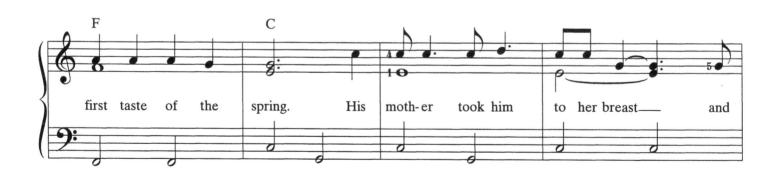

first taste of the spring. His moth - er took him to her breast___ and

soft - ly she did sing: Oh,_____ oh, Mon -

tan - a, give this child_ a home._ Give him the love of a good

fam - 'ly and a wom-an of his own._ Give him a fire in his

heart, give him a light in his eyes. Give him the wild wind for a broth -

er and the wild_____ Mon - tan - a skies._

Additional Lyrics

2. His mother died that summer, he never learned to cry.
   He never knew his father, he never did ask why.
   And he never knew the answers that would make an easy way.
   But he learned to know the wilderness and to be a man that way.

3. His mother's brother took him in to his family and his home,
   Gave him a hand that he could lean on and a strength to call his own.
   And he learned to be a farmer, and he learned to love the land.
   And he learned to read the seasons, and he learned to make a stand. *(To Chorus)*

4. On the eve of his twenty-first birthday he set out on his own.
   He was thirty years and runnin' when he found his way back home.
   Ridin' a storm across the mountains and an achin' in his heart,
   Said he came to turn the pages and to make a brand-new start.

5. Now, he never told the story of the time that he was gone.
   Some say he was a lawyer, some say he was a john.
   There was somethin' in the city that he said he couldn't breathe,
   And there was somethin' in the country that he said he couldn't leave. *(To Chorus)*

6. Now, some say he was crazy, some are glad he's gone.
   But some of us will miss him and we'll try to carry on.
   Giving a voice to the forest, giving a voice to the dawn,
   Giving a voice to the wilderness and the land that he lived on. *(To Chorus)*

For You

Words and Music by
John Denver

Just the words of a love song, _____ just the beat of my

heart, just the pledge__ of my life, __

my love, for you.
rit. *a tempo* *rit.*

Never A Doubt

Words and Music by
John Denver

per- ate morn - ings.   Nev- er a doubt,— there was nev- er a doubt— in my

mind.   I sup- pose

there have been times— when you felt
there are some peo - ple who nev-

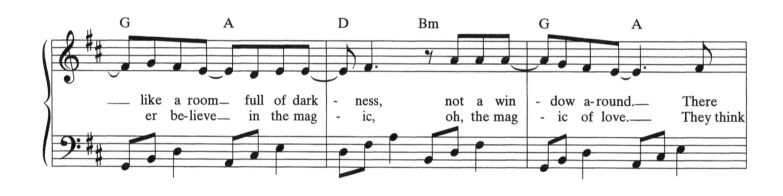

— like a room— full of dark - ness,   not a win - dow a-round.— There
er be-lieve— in the mag - ic,   oh, the mag - ic of love.— They think

must have been mo - ments you   felt you were tru - ly a- lone.—
noth- ing is pre - cious and   life is just pleas- ure and pain.—

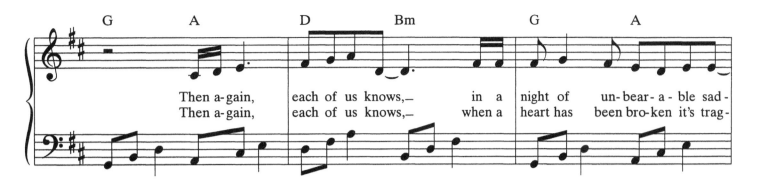

Then a-gain, each of us knows,— in a night of un-bear-a-ble sad-
Then a-gain, each of us knows,— when a heart has been bro-ken it's trag-

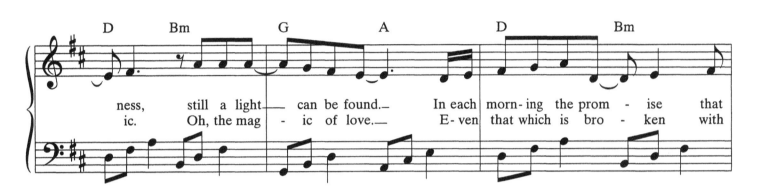

ness, still a light— can be found.— In each morn-ing the prom - ise that
ic. Oh, the mag - ic of love.— E- ven that which is bro - ken with

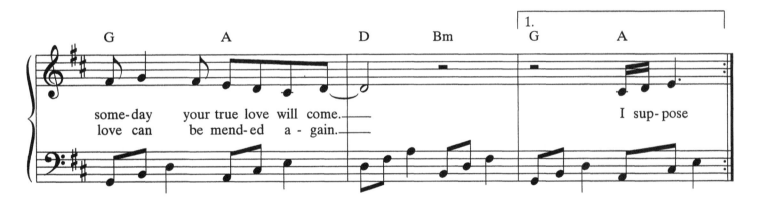

1.

some-day your true love will come.—
love can be mend-ed a - gain.— I sup-pose

2.

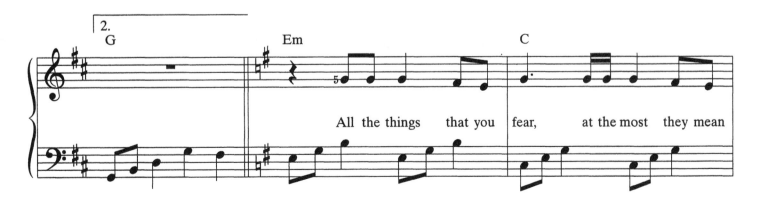

All the things that you fear, at the most they mean

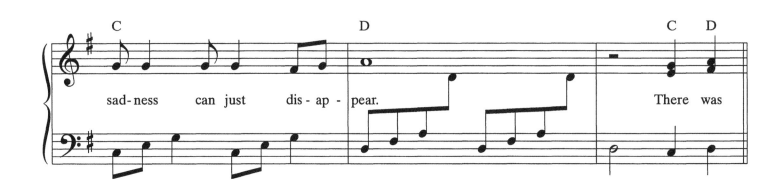

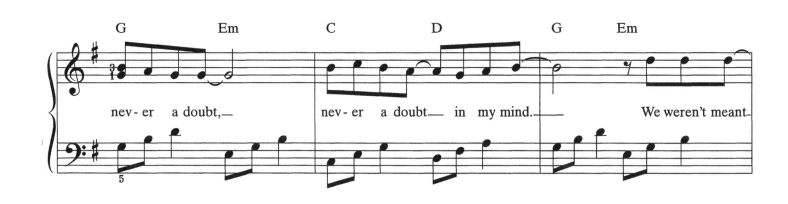

Leaving On A Jet Plane

Words and Music by
John Denver

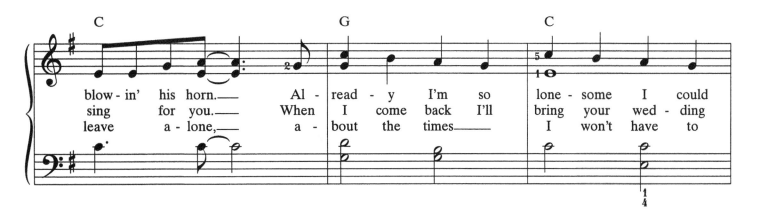

blow - in' his horn.___ Al - read - y I'm so
sing for you.___ When I come back I'll
leave a - lone,___ a - bout the times___

die.___ So kiss me and smile for me.___
ring.___ So kiss me and smile for me.___
say:___ Kiss me and smile for me.___

lone - some I could
bring your wed - ding
I won't have to

Tell me that___ you'll wait for me.___ Hold me like___ you'll nev - er let me

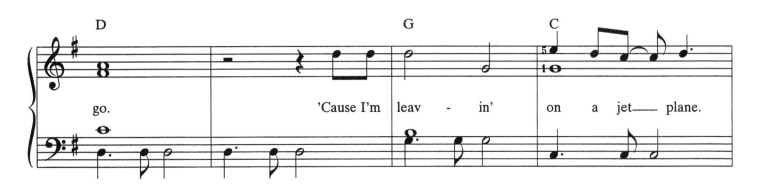

go. 'Cause I'm leav - in' on a jet___ plane.

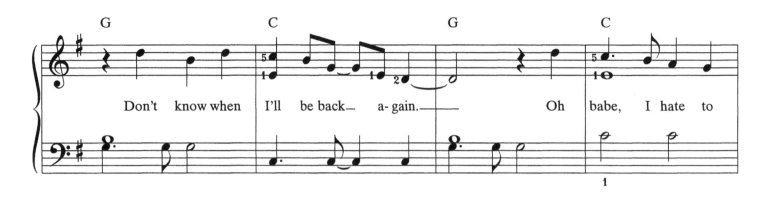

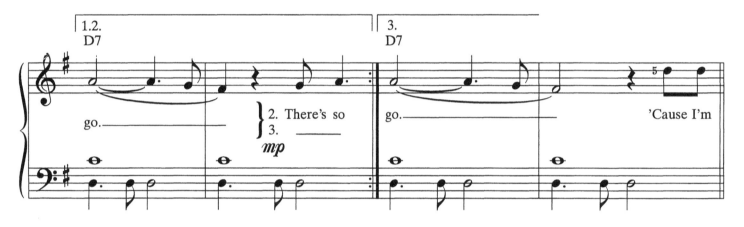

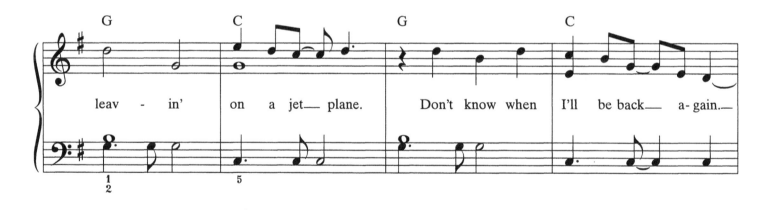